Does He Hear my prayer?

the process and procedure

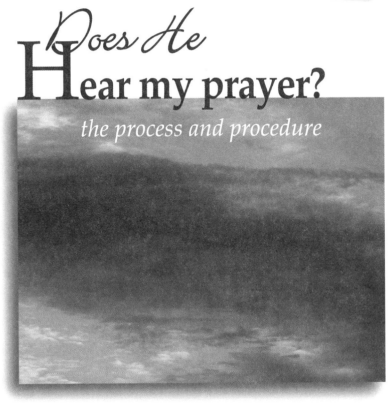

Book 4 of the '89 Basics Series

Prayer is the divinely developed system of communication, invented by God and given to believers only. Learn the correct process and procedure for prayer as stated in Scripture. As believers, we are commanded to pray.

Joe Griffin

**Joe Griffin
Media Ministries**

This book is edited from the lectures and
unpublished notes of Joe Griffin.

For a complete listing of available MP3s and publications,
see our website at: www.joegriffin.org

Joe Griffin Media Ministries
1821 South River Road
St. Charles, MO 63303-4124
USA
www.joegriffin.org
e-mail: jgmm@joegriffin.org

Photography of Joe Griffin (back cover) by Gary Knight.

Cover design by Patti Stanfield.

Cover photography ©2005 Clayton Stanfield

Printed in the United States of America

ISBN 0-9760775-3-1

Contents

Dedication iv

Preface v

Acknowledgments vi

Introduction 1

Chapter One: The Doctrine of Prayer 3
   Introduction 3
   Biblical Vocabulary for Prayer 4
   Analysis of the Four Paragraphs of Biblical Prayer 10
   Proper Prayer Content 19
   Special Prayers 22
   Why Prayers Are Not Answered .37

Chapter Two: Review - Ten Reasons Why Prayer
Goes Unanswered 54

Chapter Three: Review of Doctrines 55

Scripture Index 63

Subject Index 66

End Notes . . . . .Inside Back Cover

Dedication

Every professional has a mentor. An apprentice learns his trade from a master and I have had the privilege of learning the hermeneutics of dispensational, pretribulational, premillennial, infralapsarian theology from the preeminent theologian of the twentieth century, Rev. Robert B. Thieme, Jr., who was the pastor of Berachah Church in Houston, Texas, from 1950-2003. His advances in the literal-grammatical-historical method of biblical analysis produced cutting-edge expositions of God's immutable truth to believers throughout the world. His due diligence in studying and teaching the Word of God for over five decades led myriads to spiritual maturity and prepared a host of men with the gift of pastor-teacher to present Bible doctrine to congregations across the United States and abroad. The doctrinal content of this series of books reflects these dynamic teachings from which I have benefited as pastor of Grace Doctrine Church. It is from enduring devotion and continuing gratitude that I dedicate this series to Robert B. Thieme, Jr.

Preface

Before you begin your Bible study, if you are a believer in the Lord Jesus Christ, be sure you have named your sins privately to God the Father.

> If we confess our [known] sins, He is faithful and righteous to cleanse us from all [unknown, or forgotten sins] unrighteousness. (1 John 1:9)

You will then be in fellowship with God, filled with the Holy Spirit, and ready to learn Bible doctrine from the Word of God.

> "God is spirit, and those who worship Him must worship in [the filling of the] spirit and [biblical] truth." (John 4:24)

If you have never personally believed in the Lord Jesus Christ as your Savior, the issue is not naming your sins. The issue is faith alone in Christ alone.

> "He who believes in the Son has eternal life; but he who does not obey [the command to believe in the Son shall not see life, but the wrath of God abides on him." (John 3:36)

Acknowledgments

The publication of this series of books on the basic doctrines of the Christian faith is the result of popular demand. Without the appeals of so many people who have listened to the audiotape series, this project would never have been considered. Bringing it to fruition required the diligent assistance of a number of faithful people.

Years ago, the original class notes were lost in a computer disk crash. Modern publishing requires that manuscripts be provided in digital format. Carole Allen, a member of Grace Doctrine Church, took on the task of restoring the lost documents from the original hard copy and without her help the venture would never have gotten off the ground.

Patti Stanfield of Stanfield Designs in Wildwood, Missouri, did a masterful job of preparing the restored data for publication according to standards from *The Chicago Manual of Style.* The professional appearance of this series is due to Patti's hard work. I appreciate her patience with me as I missed several deadlines along the way.

Finally, my picture on the back cover does as much grace to the subject as photographic expertise can provide. I am privileged to have had my countenance struck by one of the country's leading photographers, Gary Knight of Blue Ridge, Georgia. A fellow member of the Berachah Battalion, Gary went out of his way to come to St. Charles to do the shoot.

Appreciation is extended to Lindenwood University of St. Charles, Missouri, (www.lindenwood.edu) for allowing us to use Boonesfield Village's Old Peace Chapel at its Daniel Boone Campus in Defiance, Missouri, for the photo sessions.

Joe Griffin, Pastor
Grace Doctrine Church
St. Charles, Missouri
May 2010

INTRODUCTION
About the '89 Basics Series

You are about to delve into **Book Four** of the *'89 Basics Series,* a series of basic instructional biblical studies.This study is designed for two categories of people:

(1)   Those who are not familiar with Christianity but would like to become oriented to its basic beliefs and doctrines.

(2)   Those who already consider themselves to be Christians but have to this point not been entirely clear on what principles are basic to the Christian faith.

We affectionately refer to church as God's "Classroom for Christianity." I am the teacher. The textbook is the Bible. You are the student.

In our course of study you will find it helpful to have a Bible handy. If you do not own one, may I suggest that you purchase the *Oxford Scofield Study Bible.* It is available in the King James Version and the New International Version.

This volume is part of a four-book series that contains my class notes for the *'89 Basics Series.* You may wish to use it as a study guide while listening to the series on audiotape or MP3 recordings, or study it independently. Please note that the program can be used effectively with either books *or* tapes or in a combination of books *and* tapes. As you read through the textual material, reference will be made to direct you to listen to the audio media should you desire. The corresponding lesson number will be noted as shown below.

BAS-01

If you would like to obtain other books in this series or the recorded series, please provide your mailing address, indicating the book title and/or your desired media format (audiotape or MP3) and mail it to the address indicated on the inside back cover of this book. Entitled *End Notes*, this information states our Financial Policy and provides ordering information for those who desire to continue the series or proceed with further studies.

CHAPTER ONE
The Doctrine of Prayer

I. Introduction

1. Prayer is the unique prerogative of the royal priesthood.

2. It is the divinely developed system of communication between the royal family and God the Father.

3. This system is the invention of God and is given to believers only. It includes provisions for submitting requests to Him while engaged in the Angelic Conflict.

4. These prayer requests come in two major categories:

   a. Intercession—prayer for others.
   b. Petition—prayer for oneself.

5. There is a correct process and procedure for prayer stated in the Scriptures:

   a. All prayer is to be directed to the Father. Matthew 6:9; John 17:1; Ephesians 5:20*a*

   b. Next comes content beginning with rebound, followed by thanksgiving, intercession and petition. We will examine all of these paragraphs later.

   c. All prayer is to be submitted in the name of Jesus Christ. John 14:13-14; Ephesians 5:20*b*

6. No prayer is processed which is not offered in the filling of the Holy Spirit. Ephesians 6:18; Jude 20

7. We are commanded to pray.

   1 Thessalonians 5:17 - Pray on a continually consistent basis.

8. Prayer is an offensive weapon in the Angelic Conflict. It is designed to solve problems before they occur, not as an after-the-fact problem-solving device.

9. Effective intercessory prayer requires thinking. Spiritual thinking is doctrinal thinking and requires concentration.

10. For the baby believer, effective prayer is linked to two problem-solving devices: rebound and the Faith-Rest Technique.

11. As the believer advances in his spiritual maturity, he will place less emphasis on his petitions and greater emphasis on his intercessions.

II. Biblical Vocabulary for Prayer

1. ὁμολογέω, *homologeô* - Confess; acknowledge; cite.

   1 John 1:9 - If we confess (*homologeô*) our sins, He is faithful and just and will forgive us our sins and purify us from all unrighteousness.

2. εὐχαριστία, *eucharistia* - Thanksgivings

   a. Those who receive grace gifts from fellow believers should direct thanks to God in prayer.

2 Corinthians 9:11 - You will be made rich in every way so that you can be generous on every occasion and through us your generosity will result in thanksgiving (*eucharistia*) to God.

b. This does not mean you are discourteous to those who assist you through grace. Good manners require that you thank the person who was motivated to assist you. Thanksgivings to God is a function of private prayer.

c. Thanksgivings to God must become a regular portion of your prayer life.

Ephesians 5:20 - Always giving thanks to God the Father for everything in the name of our Lord Jesus Christ.

d. No matter what difficulties you face you are always in the plan of God. God has made provision for every difficulty in life. Grace demands that you recognize this fact in the form of thanksgiving.

Philippians 4:6 - Stop worrying about anything but in everything by prayer and petition after thanksgivings (*eucharistia*), let your requests be made known unto God.

3. ἔντευξις, *enteuxis* - Intercession; means to intercede; to act on behalf of another.

a. Jesus Christ is seated at the right hand of God in heaven. He currently serves as our Advocate, or our Defense Attorney, defending us against accusations from Satan when we commit personal sin.

b. Our Lord's function as advocate is that of intercessor. He affirms to the Father in intercessory prayer on our behalf that the sins cited by Satan were borne by Him on the cross.

c. Such testimony is always sustained by the Father and the case against the believer is nol-prossed by His justice under the principle of double jeopardy.

Revelation 12:10 - Then I heard a loud voice in heaven say, "Now have come the salvation and the power and the kingdom of our God and the authority of Christ. For the accuser of our fellow believers, who accuses them day and night, has been hurled down."

1 John 2:1*b* - If any man sins, we have an Advocate—One Who speaks to the Father in our defense—Jesus Christ the Righteous One.

Hebrews 7:25 - Therefore, Jesus Christ is able to save for eternity those who come to God through Him, because He always lives to intercede (*enteuxis*) for them.

d. The Holy Spirit also offers intercessory prayer to the Father on our behalf.

Romans 8:27 - The Father, Who searches our right lobes knows what the thinking of the Holy Spirit is because according to God, He makes intercession (*enteuxis*) on behalf of the saints.

4. δέησις, *deêsis* - Petition; Supplication (KJV); entreaty. Petition based on immediate need. A thing asked for in the sense of desire or request. To ask for oneself.

Ephesians 6:18*a* - Pray in the filling of the Holy Spirit on all occasions with all kinds of prayers and petitions (*deêsis*).

1 Peter 3:12 - "The eyes of the Lord are on the righteous and His ears are attentive to their petition (*deêsis*)."

Philippians 4:6 - Stop worrying about anything but in everything by prayer and petition (*deêsis*) after thanksgivings (*eucharistia*), let your requests (*aitêma*) be made known unto God.

5. αἴτημα, *aitêma* - Request

    I John 5:15 - If we know that He hears us—whatever we ask—we know that we have the requests (*aitêma*) we asked of Him.

    a. *Aitêma* is the word which designates the specifics of your prayer. Your requests may be expressed for yourself or for others.

6. προσευχή, *proseuchê* - Prayer. Used to cover prayer in general and may refer to any of the specific areas of prayer.

7. There are several verses in which these terms are used together. By examining them we are able to construct God's desired process and procedure for our prayers to Him.

    a. Ephesians 6:18 - By means of all prayer (*proseuchê*) and petition (*deêsis*) pray at all times in the filling of the Holy Spirit, being alert to keep praying for all the saints.

b. Philippians 4:6 - Stop worrying about anything but in everything by prayer (*proseuchê*) and petition (*deêsis*) after thanksgiving (*eucharistia*), let your requests (*aitêma*) be made known unto God.

c. Let's review a couple of words here:

Aitêma means "request" and is a general term for the content of your prayer. It refers to your specific, individual requests in either intercession or petition.

Proseuchê means "prayer" and is a general term for the categories of prayer.

d. A helpful grammatical key in interpreting prayer passages goes as follows:

Whenever the general word for prayer categories is stated, *proseuchê*, and the word for "petition", *deêsis*, is linked to it by a conjunction then *proseuchê* stands for intercession.

e. Now let's note our two verses again:

Ephesians 6:18 - By means of all intercession (*proseuchê*) and petition (*deêsis*) ...

Philippians 4:6 - Stop worrying about anything but in everything by intercession (*proseuchê*) and petition (*deêsis*) after thanksgivings (*eucharistia*)...

8. From our passages, we are now able to develop the correct biblical outline for our prayers:

a. Salutation: Father   πατήρ, *Pater*
b. Rebound: Confession   ὁμολογέω, *homologeô*
c. Prologue: Thanksgiving   εὐχαριστία, *eucharistia*

d. Meditation: Intercession   ἐντευξις, *enteuxis*
e. Invocation: Petition   δεήσις, *deêsis*
f. Authority: In the name
   of Jesus Christ   ὀνομα, *onoma*

9. In no way is this to be viewed as some sort of ritual in which, if you get the order right your prayers will be answered.

BAS-45

10. What it demonstrates is the proper mental attitude for a person addressing the God of the universe.

11. It is the Father's desire that you address your prayers to Him and you honor that request with the vocative, "Father."

12. It is imperative that our prayers be expressed under the filling of the Holy Spirit inside the divine power system. This is accomplished through rebound.

13. A proper grace mental attitude is expressed by taking the time to thank God for His ongoing provisions and blessings before making any further requests of Him.

14. Romans 12:10 commands us to "make it a matter of honor to show preference to others." Recognition of this mandate is reflected in our prayers when we place our intercessions for others ahead of petitions for ourselves.

15. And we have noted how Scripture tells us that the authority by which we are allowed to pray is through Christ. We express that by closing our prayers, "in the name of Jesus Christ."

III. Analysis of the Four Paragraphs of Biblical Prayer

A. The ὁμολογέω, *homologeô* Paragraph: Rebound

    1. We have studied this paragraph in detail earlier in our *'89 Basics Series*.

    2. We are fully aware of its necessity and its indispensability with regard to our ability to execute the Christian way of life.

    3. Therefore, we will not undertake a review of this paragraph other than to note several pertinent passages: Psalm 66:18; John 9:31; 1 Corinthians 11:31; 1 John 1:9.

B. The εὐχαριστία, *eucharistia* Paragraph: Thanksgivings

    1. This word is a compound of εὐ-, *eu-* well; good; proper; and χαρίζομαι, *charizomai*, a mental attitude of joy.

    2. Literally you have a thankful mental attitude manifest by an expression of gratitude.

    3. Proper thanksgiving is only possible through knowledge of the plan of God, His policy of grace and His purpose of blessing.

    4. Thanksgiving is the act of expressing gratitude to God based on knowledge of His Word.

    5. Ignorance of the Word means ignorance of God and therefore, no proper understanding of the grace of God.

    6. The privilege of going to God in prayer is not

something man initiated.

7. In eternity past, God in His grace chose to allow men the option of communication with Him.

8. As a royal priest, you have the unique prerogative of prayer whether you utilize it or not.

9. Unfortunately, in our land of cornucopia, far too few have this mental attitude of thanksgiving.

10. 2 Timothy 3:1 -Mark this: There will be terrible times in the last days.

> Verse 2 - People will be lovers of themselves, lovers of money, boastful, arrogant, abusive, disobedient to their parents, unthankful, unholy.

> Romans 1:21 - Although they knew God, they neither glorified Him as God nor gave thanks to Him...

11. When we pray, we should pause and be mindful that it is only through His grace that we are allowed to speak directly with Him in the first place.

12. The use of thanksgiving in plural in Philippians 4:6 indicates that we are already the beneficiaries of God's abundant grace.

13. The more we love God the more we become aware of our blessings and thus more motivated to offer our thanks to Him.

14. Personal Love for God motivates unconditional

love toward mankind with resultant gratitude toward both.

15. This virtue love toward both produces a mental stability, which enables the believer to face every circumstance with an attitude of thanksgiving.

16. 1 Thessalonians 5:18 - In everything give thanks for this is the will of God for you in Christ Jesus.

17. Once you become spiritually self-sustaining, your life is characterized by contentment and a mental attitude of thanksgiving.

    Philippians 4:11 - I am not saying this because I am in need, for I have learned to be content whatever the circumstances.

       Verse 12 - I know what it is to be in need and I know what it is to have plenty. I have learned the secret of being content in any and every situation, whether well fed or hungry, whether living in plenty or in want.

       Verse 13 - I can do everything through the enabling power of the Holy Spirit Who keeps pouring the power into me.

C. The ἐντευχις, *enteuxis* Paragraph: Intercession

    1. This type of prayer is a request to God for His assistance, provision or guidance for others.

    2. There are many passages where this function can be seen:

        Ephesians 1:16 - I do not cease giving thanks for

you and I make mention of you in my prayers.

Verse 17 - In order that the God of our Lord Jesus Christ, the Father of glory, may give you a lifestyle of wisdom and revelation about Him through *epignôsis* doctrine.

Verse 18 - I also pray that the eyes of your soul may be enlightened so that you may know what is the hope of His calling, the riches of the glory of His inheritance for the saints.

Philippians 1:3 - I thank my God every time I remember you.

Verse 4 - In all my prayers for all of you, I always pray with joy.

Verse 5 - Because of your partnership in the Gospel from the first day until now,...

Verse 6 - ...being confident of this, that He Who began a good work in you will carry it to completion until the day of Christ.

Colossians 1:7 - Epaphras gave us a written report about your unconditional love which the Holy Spirit produces in you.

Verse 9 - Because of this unconditional love, from the day on which we heard, we have not stopped praying for you and have constantly been asking (making intercessory prayer), in order that you might be filled with the knowledge of His will by means of all wisdom and spiritual understanding.

Verse 10 - That you conduct yourselves worthy of the Lord, seeking to please Him in every way, bearing fruit by every good work, always making progress in the sphere of the knowledge that comes from the source of God.

Verse 11 - That you might be constantly made strong by means of every enabling power (in keeping with His sovereign power which has His essence as its source) in order that you might always have endurance, stability and patience with joy;

Verse 12 - constantly being thankful to the Father, the One Who made it possible for you to share in the inheritance of the saints in the sphere of the light.

3. Note some of the things Paul prays for in this Colossians passage:

   1. That the believers in the Colossian church might be filled with *epignôsis* doctrine concerning the will of God. (Verse 9)

   2. That they would execute the Christian way of life, which is how you conduct yourself in a manner worthy of the Lord. (Verse 10)

   3. That they would show positive volition toward the plan of God: "seeking to please Him in every way." (Verse 10)

   4. That they would produce divine good: "bearing fruit by every good work." (Verse 10)

   5. That they would continue their advance

toward spiritual maturity: "always making progress in the sphere of knowledge." (Verse 10)

6. That they would utilize the enabling power of the Holy Spirit: "that you might constantly be made strong by means of every enabling power." (Verse 11)

7. That through this power they might "have endurance, stability and patience with happiness." (Verse 11)

8. That they would be constantly thankful to God for these assets. (Verse 12)

9. That they might be motivated by the prospect of future and eternal blessings available to those who execute the plan of God through spiritual growth: "the One Who made it possible for you to share in the inheritance of the saints in the sphere of light." (Verse 12)

4. The most powerful prayer you can pray for others is that they might be led and directed by God's grace to the status of spiritual maturity.

BAS-46

5. The prayer/bulletin of a local church should be designed to provide a ready-made prayer list.

6. Other prayers one may offer in the field of Intercession will come up later under the section on Special Prayers.

D. The δεήσις, *deêsis* Paragraph: Petition

1. This is a prayer request for your own personal needs and desires.

2. Usually the prayers of petition have to do with a failure to understand or utilize the problem-solving devices.

3. Most problems in life can be handled by the application of doctrine.

4. When one prays for something to occur it is usually an attempt to solve a problem.

5. First of all, problems must be analyzed from the standpoint of God's plan; secondly, from the standpoint of your status in that plan.

6. Are you current on rebound; have you fallen victim to your own poor decisions; are you experiencing suffering or blessing through People, System, Thought or Disaster Testings?

7. Are you utilizing the biblical problem-solving devices available to handle these situations? Rebound removes discipline and turns your suffering into blessing.

8. Unconditional love solves People testing. 1 Corinthians 13:4-8

9. Recall and application of doctrine solves Thought testing. 2 Corinthians 10:

   Verse 4 - For the weapons of our warfare (spiritual) are not of human origin but are of divine power to destroy fortifications (cosmic thinking);

Verse 5 - To assaulting and demolishing (with Bible doctrine) speculations (cosmic thinking, human viewpoint thinking) and every obstacle of arrogance against the knowledge of God; even making a prisoner of every thought (contrary to Word of God) to the obedience of Christ;

Verse 6 - Holding in readiness (maximum doctrine as an instant reaction force) to punish all deviation when your obedience has been fulfilled.

10. Notice that the solution to Thought Testing was a high inventory of doctrinal ideas learned from many Bible classes.

11. System Testing: A system is an organization composed of people under the command of other people functioning under a policy which is designed to fulfill a specific objective.

12. The policy and the objective of the organization can cause System Testing.

13. The policy may be unreasonable. It may conflict with your own personal norms and standards or it may be imprudent, irresponsible, reckless or irrelevant.

14. The objective may be unreasonable or even impossible to attain. There may be lack of ability, equipment, or budget. The objective may conflict with your norms and standards.

15. The Faith-Rest Technique solves the problems presented by policy and objective while uncondi-

tional love takes care of authority.

16. You therefore utilize rebound, you claim promises and apply doctrine. Further, you pray for those in authority over you.

17. A major passage on System Testing is Colossians 3:22-4:2.

18. There are three categories of disaster testing:

    a. Personal disaster, which is designed as suffering for acceleration of spiritual growth.

    b. Warning discipline because of cosmic living.

    c. Historical disaster related to the bad decisions of others in which you are involved by association.

19. The solution to disaster testing involves the Faith-Rest Technique:

    a. Claim a promise, i.e., 1 Corinthians 10:13 (look it up)

    b. Concentrate on the Plan of God and Essence of God Rationales (look them up).

    c. Come to the doctrinal conclusion that if God is in control of the situation, you don't have to sweat it.

20. There may be quite a number of things you need to be physically doing in the application of doctrine to your circumstances, but worry is not one of them.

21. It is not necessary to pray for logistics since they are guaranteed. You do not pray for miracles or healing since these are for a previous dispensation.

22. Petitions should emphasize your function in the plan of God and your duty to glorify Him in the Angelic Conflict.

23. If you take care of business, God will take care of you.

IV. Proper Prayer Content

A. Introduction

1. All prayer, in order to be effective, must be composed within the framework of orthodox doctrine.

   John 15:7 - "If you abide in Me (fellowship) and My words abide in you (*epignôsis* doctrine resident in the soul), ask whatever you wish and it shall be done for your advantage."

2. God is the Inventor of prayer. He establishes the rules and regulations for its use by select members of the human race.

3. We have noted our divine authorization to approach God in prayer as a prerogative of the royal priesthood.

4. We have learned the proper agenda for prayer: Confession, thanksgivings, intercessions and petition.

5. We have identified proper prayer protocol. It is addressed to the Father, in the name of the Son

and in the power of the Holy Spirit.

6. We understand that our prayers must go through channels: The Holy Spirit assists us in the development and presentation of our prayers (Ephesians 6:18); Jesus Christ as our Intercessor authorizes their presentation to the Father (Hebrews 7:25); and God the Father processes the prayers so offered (1 John 5:14).

7. We have also noted that the correct agenda of prayer organizes and motivates the proper mental attitude for prayer.

8. However, all of this is meaningless if the *content* of our prayers violates the guidelines revealed in Scripture.

9. The specifics of your prayers are unique and personal to you, however they must fall within certain guidelines.

B. Proper Prayer Must Be Composed from Doctrine Resident in Your Soul

1. Mark 11:24 - "I say to you, all things for which you ask and pray, believe that you will receive them and they shall be given to you."

2. Here we see the word for "believe": πιστεύω, *pisteuô*. It means to place your faith in that which is believed, i.e., Bible doctrine.

3. Your requests must entail those things, which agree with the revealed will of God and His perfect plan.

4. To construct your prayers from doctrine you know means that requests fall in line with His will and plan.

5. A basic question one should ask himself regarding his petitions should be, "Is what I am about to ask for necessary before I can do God's will?"

6. To pray a prayer that you know is incongruous with the plan of God must generate doubt and therefore unbelief.

7. Example: To pray for God to override one's volition and save an unbeliever, violates the plan and will of God and cannot be answered.

8. To ask the ability to do God's will but through extraordinary means, is a violation of the plan and will of God.

9. Example: To pray that yourself or someone will be healed of cancer; or to pray for the gift of miracles and healing so you can heal yourself or someone else.

10. Under the filling of the Holy Spirit, the believer will formulate a prayer from doctrine resident in his soul and thus ask for only those things, which promote the plan and will of God.

C. Maximum Effectiveness of Prayer is Dependent Upon Maximum Doctrine in the Soul

1. John 15:7 - "If you abide in Me (fellowship through the filling of the Holy Spirit) ask whatever you wish and it shall be done for your advantage."

2. The more doctrine you know the more cognizant you become of the plan and will of God.

3. Consequently. The more doctrine you know the more powerful your prayer life becomes.

V. Special Prayers

A. Over Meals

1. 1 Timothy 4:4 - For everything created by God is good for food and nothing is to be rejected if it is received with thanksgivings.

   Verse 5 - For it is sanctified by means of the word of God and prayer.

2. Your "blessing" should include a statement of thanksgiving, followed by a petition that the food be sanctified.

3. The word for sanctified is ἁγιάζω, *hagiazô* and means to be set apart; to be separated from evil.

   present - Perfective; denotes continuation of results. The food although it may be somehow dangerous, the danger is removed and the food is actually turned into nourishment.

   passive - The food receives the action of the verb and is thus set apart and sanctified.

   indicative - Declarative; a statement of biblical fact.

4. What is it that causes this sanctification process to occur? Two things are mentioned:

1. διά λόγος, *dia logos* - through the agency of the Word of God, and;

2. ἐντευξις, *enteuxis* - Prayer; intercession. You do not pray for yourself but rather for the food.

5. This verse tells us that God has set apart everything which He created as good for food.

   Genesis 1:29 - God said, "I give you every seed-bearing plant on the face of the whole earth and every tree that has fruit with seed in it. They will be yours for food."

6. This was the sanctification of vegetable life. The "animal rights" activists quit reading here. They fail to continue on to Genesis 9:

   Verse 2 - "The fear and dread of you will fall upon all the beasts of the earth and all the birds of the air, upon every creature that moves along the ground and upon all the fish of the sea; they are given into your hands.

   Verse 3 - "Everything that lives and moves will be food for you. Just as I gave you the green plants, I now give you everything."

   BAS-47

B. For Those in Authority

1. 1 Timothy 2:1 - First of all, I urge (παρακαλέω, *parakaleô*: To summon someone to your side to give them commands or orders, thus this takes on the impact of a command) that petitions (*deêsis*), prayers (*proseuchê*), intercessions

(*enteuxis*) and thanksgivings (*eucharistia*), be made on behalf of everyone—

Verse 2 - ...for kings (ὑπέρ βασιλεύς, *huper basileus*: Refers to highest governmental authority, i.e., president) and to all who are in authority (refers to all other establishment officials) in order that we may lead an undisturbed (outer tranquility) and peaceable life (inner tranquility) in all godliness (spiritual maturity) and integrity.

Verse 3 - This is good and acceptable to our Savior God.

2. It is considered important by our Savior, Who controls history on behalf of the Pivot, that we pray for establishment authorities.

3. It is His desire that just government control the affairs of all mankind.

4. Good leadership produces tranquility for the client nation:

    1. Peace is maintained against any external aggression by strong military preparedness.

    2. Peace is maintained against any internal revolution by a strong system of jurisprudence.

5. The resultant tranquility guarantees maximum effectiveness for both evangelism and Bible teaching.

C. For the Unbeliever

    1. It is very important to understand that the voli-

tion of the unbeliever cannot be overruled by either God or your prayers.

2. Proper prayer for the unbeliever acknowledges this fact and thus makes an appeal to the essence of God.

3. We should ask that God in His sovereignty would prepare the target to receive Gospel information under the best possible circumstances.

4. These circumstances would include all that is necessary for the target to give the Gospel a hearing and to do so under the most objective of circumstances.

5. Our prayers should therefore appeal to the justice of God to bring the target to a point of maximum mental receptiveness.

6. This can be brought home to the target by personal disaster to himself or others—poor health, illness, accident, disease, loss of property or loved ones.

7. Disaster is many times a way of focusing a person on what is top priority in life.

8. When a person's priorities are removed he is then more likely to become aware of other, more important priorities.

9. Prayers for the unbeliever must center around three factors:

   a. That the target might be exposed to the Gospel and thus afforded an opportunity to respond;

b. That he would have a clear understanding of the issue so presented that there would be no confusion regarding the ramifications of his decision;

c. That God would prepare him in such a way that when he is presented the Gospel his mental attitude would be as objective as possible.

10. The emphasis on volition as a necessity for salvation in a context of prayer for the unbeliever is the subject of Romans 9-11.

11. I would like to very quickly summarize this passage in order to accomplish two things:

a. That prayers for the unbeliever must acknowledge volitional choice on the part of the target, and

b. That Romans 10:9-10 does not require any public profession of faith directed toward a congregation, other Christians or to church officials.

Romans 9-11:

1. Chapters 9, 10, and 11 of Romans is a parenthesis inserted between chapters 8 and 12.

2. Paul, who called himself the Hebrew of Hebrews in Philippians 3:5 has a tremendous concern for those fellow Jews who refuse to accept his presentation of Jesus as their Messiah.

3. He notes that they still consider the keeping of the Mosaic Law through its rituals and works as the way to salvation and eternal life.

4. This parenthesis is addressed specifically to Jewish unbelievers.

5. Chapter 9 speaks of Israel's selection by God in the past. Chapter 10 speaks of Israel's rejection by God in the present. Chapter 11 speaks of Israel's acceptance by God in the future.

6. In Chapter 9, Paul distinguishes between the racial Jew, who has rejected Christ as Messiah, and the spiritual Jew, who has accepted Him.

7. The racial Jew seeks salvation and imputed righteousness through the Law, whereas the spiritual Jew and Gentile acquire it through faith alone.

8. Paul is distraught over the fact that so many of his racial family have rejected the righteousness which is granted through grace and instead continue to work, through keeping the law, to earn their righteousness.

9. Romans 9:30 - Therefore, to what conclusion are we forced? That the Gentiles who did not strive for self-righteousness, have attained divine righteousness, that is, the righteousness which is from the source of faith in Christ.

Verse 31 - But Israel, who pursued after righteousness based on the Law, has not attained the purpose of the Law (which is salvation.)

Verse 32 - Why? Because they did not pursue it (righteousness) by means of an act of faith but rather as if it were by means of many works. They stumbled over the Stumbling Stone.

Verse 33 - As it stands written, (Isaiah 8:14; 26:16) "Behold, I lay a foundation in Zion, a Stumbling Stone (Jesus Christ) and a Rock of offense, nevertheless, the one believing in Him will not be disappointed."

10. Paul points out that only the Jew who believes in Jesus Christ will not be disappointed at His Second Advent.

11. The pattern of salvation for all mankind including Jews is demonstrated by Abraham in Romans 4:

Verse 1 - Therefore, what do we conclude that Abraham our human father has obtained?

Verse 2 - Assuming that Abraham has been justified by means of works, he has a basis for boasting but definitely not before God.

Verse 3 - For what does the Scripture say? (Genesis 15:6) "Now Abraham had believed in God and that faith was credited to him for righteousness."

Verse 4 - But to him who works for salvation, his wages are not credited according to grace but according to debt.

Verse 5 - But to him who does not work for salvation but believes in Him who justifies the unbeliever, his faith receives credit for the imputation of divine righteousness.

12. In Chapter 10, Paul begins by teaching the failure of Israel to accept Jesus as its Messiah in verse 1-11.

13. The remainder of the chapter demonstrates the resultant failure of Israel to function as a missionary nation.

14. He opens the commentary by pointing out that self-righteousness based on the works of the Law results in unbelief in Christ but that faith alone in Christ alone produces righteousness through grace.

15. Romans 10:

Verse 1 - Brethren, the motivation of my soul and my prayer to God on behalf of them (Israel) is for their salvation.

Verse 2 - For I testify they have a zeal for God but not as a result of spiritual knowledge.

Verse 3 - For not knowing the righteousness of God and seeking to establish their own righteousness, they have not been obedient to the righteousness of God.

Verse 4 - For Christ is the end of the Law resulting in righteousness for everyone who believes.

16. In Romans 10:8 Paul then puts forward the question inspired by the Deuteronomy 30:11-14 passage:

    Verse 8 - What does Deuteronomy 30:11-14 say? "The message of salvation is near you, in your mouth and in your soul." That is the message of faith which we proclaim.

17. Paul now drives home the argument to his unsaved Jewish friends in the next two verses.

18. He has reminded them of the words of Moses and now he relates them to Jesus Christ as the fulfillment of the Law.

    Romans 10:9 - Namely, if you will acknowledge with your mouth to God, "Jesus is Lord," and if you will believe in your soul that God has raised Him from the dead, you will be saved."

    Verse 10 - For you see, by means of the soul, mankind believes resulting in imputed righteousness and by means of the mouth mankind makes an acknowledgement to God about salvation.

19. Verses 9 and 10 communicate the nearness of salvation. They are a conclusion to

verse 8 which states that salvation is as near as the mouth and the soul.

20. Remember, the targets of this discourse are Jews. The emphasis is not so much on the *mechanics* of salvation as the *nearness* of salvation.

BAS-48

21. The Jews are committed to a works system for salvation and reject faith as the valid means of acquiring righteousness.

22. Consequently, they are involved in functions for salvation which are outside themselves and involve things, animals, people and ritual.

23. Paul is pointing out with Moses that salvation is within the soul of man not without; it is something which may be stated to God with the mouth, not through ritual.

24. Salvation is the complete understanding that one is forgiven of his sins because of what Christ did on the cross.

25. This understanding is reached in the soul.

26. The Gospel enters the soul and is understood there through the enabling power of the Holy Spirit.

27. Understanding is acquired through utilization of a vocabulary which forms sentences which convey thought.

28. When one truly understands salvation, he is able to reduce that understanding to words in a prayer to God.

29. Consequently, when a person acquires a large enough vocabulary to understand the Gospel, he has not only the power to understand but also the ability to recite that belief to God in a salvation prayer.

30. It is arrogance to think that acknowledgement of your belief in Christ to other people is what saves you.

31. Other people can't save you. Only God can save you, and that salvation based solely on your belief in what Christ did on the cross.

32. The phrase, "Jesus is Lord," in verse 9 had great impact on the Jews of Paul's day.

33. The word for "Lord" in the Greek is *Kurios* and is equivalent to the Hebrew Jehovah.

34. To the Jew, such a statement meant they believed that Jesus was the Messiah (the God/Man Redeemer) promised to Israel.

35. This statement was to be directed to God not to others.

36. When expressed to God it is a statement of belief, when expressed to others it is a statement of the Gospel.

37. Verse 9 emphasizes the belief that Jesus is the Messiah followed by a belief that He was resurrected from the dead.

38. Verse 10 explains the cause and effect of salvation and acknowledgement:

    Verse 10*a* - For you see, by means of the soul mankind believes resulting in imputed righteousness ...

39. This volitional choice is manifested by a salvation prayer to God expressing this inward belief:

    Verse 10*b* - ... and by means of the mouth mankind makes an acknowledgement to God about salvation.

40. Paul concludes this paragraph with the summary statement:

    Verse 11 - Therefore, the Scripture says, "When anyone believes on Him, they shall not be disappointed."

41. The concept of salvation by grace through faith in Christ alone is replete throughout the New Testament. Compare Romans 10:8-11 with the following: John 3:15-16, 18, 36; 6:47; 11:25; 20:31; Acts 16:31; Romans 1:16; 3:22,28; 4:1-5; Galatians 2:16, 3:26; 1 John 5:11-13; Ephesians 2:8-9.

42. In conclusion, Romans 10:9-10 must be understood within its parenthetical context of Romans 9-11 which emphasizes the

frame of reference of the Jewish unbeliever who is very knowledgeable about the law but ignorant about grace and faith.

43. Further, we must be very cautious about any English translation which seems to add something to salvation, beyond faith alone.

44. This passage must be compared to the overwhelming evidence of other related passages. Several have just been stated.

45. To imply that salvation is by means of human works is to destroy the concept of grace.

46. Christ did all the work necessary to save our souls on the cross. All we are asked to do is believe it.

47. To add any human function as a qualification of salvation is to say that salvation is not by the grace of God but is achieved through the works of man.

48. If man may do anything to appropriate his own salvation then why is there any need for a Savior?

    Titus 3:5 - Not because of righteous things which we have done but because of His mercy He saved us.

D. For Your Enemies

1. Matthew 5:44 - "But I say to you, love your enemies and pray for those who persecute you."

2. The technique is to utilize the problem-solving device of unconditional love.

3. Your prayer should be for the person's conversion as we have just noted.

4. Your prayer should request that the person be brought to recognize his error and the need for intake of truth.

5. How God brings this to pass is none of your concern.

6. Your desire is that the individual realize he is causing problems and correct it through positive volition toward the Gospel and toward doctrine.

7. You must allow God to take care of all the details.

E. For Fellow Believers' Spiritual Adulthood

1. Philippians 1:9 - This is my prayer: That your unconditional love may abound more and more in *epignôsis* knowledge of doctrine and all discernment.

    Colossians 1:9 - Because of this unconditional love, from the day on which we heard, we have not stopped praying for you and continuing to ask, in order that you might be filled with the knowledge of His will by means of all wisdom and spiritual understanding.

2. It is easy to pray for the positive volition believer; they are involved in the upward advance toward spiritual maturity.

3. Their souls are under the consistent control of the Holy Spirit; they are motivated by maximum doctrine resident in their souls.

4. Your prayer for the positive believer is that God would continue to motivate him to pursue truth.

5. Such motivation is easy to accomplish for the positive believer:

   a. There are rewards and blessings for time and eternity.

   b. They see doctrine at work in their lives.

   c. They face challenges that are tailor-made by God for their continued motivation to press the attack.

6. Your prayer support is their artillery barrage as they fight the good fight of faith.

F. For the Communicators of Truth (Evangelists, Pastors, Missionaries)

   1. 2 Thessalonians 3:1 - Finally, fellow believers, pray for us that the message of the Lord may spread rapidly and be honored, just as it was with you.

      Hebrews 13:18 - Pray for us.

      Colossians 4:2 - Devote yourselves to prayer,

keeping alert with an attitude of thanksgiving.

> Verse 3 - Praying at the same time for us as well that God may open up to us a door for the Word that we may communicate the mystery doctrine of Christ for which doctrine I am in chains.

2. There are somewhere between 60 and 100 doctrine-oriented Bible churches in the United States. Pray for their pastors.

3. Pray for evangelists such as Gary Horton and Rick Hughes and for missionaries such as Moses Onwubiko, Ralph LaRosa and Max Klein and youth ministers such as Quentin Swafford.

4. Our prayer support of these people is a fulfill-ment of our national and international impact on the next generation.

5. Pray that these communicators might constantly be motivated to pursue truth and then accurately communicate it.

VI. Why Prayers Are Not Answered

1. Carnality and Cosmic Living

    1. Psalm 66:18 - If I regard iniquity in my heart, the Lord will not hear me.

        This is life outside the bottom circle due to uncon-fessed sin in the life. A common name for this sta-tus is being "out of fellowship."

    2. Ephesians 4:30 - Do not grieve the Holy Spirit.

This is a command for the believer to stay out of the arrogance complex of the Cosmic Systems.

3. 1 Thessalonians 5:19 - Do not quench the Holy Spirit.

    This is a command for the believer to stay out of the hatred complex of the Cosmic Systems.

2. Rejection of Divine Policy

    1. Only the Bible teaches the proper mechanics for prayer.

    2. If God did not intend for prayer to be conducted in a prescribed manner then He would not have taken the time to reveal it in Scripture.

    3. In this area, prayer fails because of three things:

        1. Failure to observe proper prayer procedure (rebound, thanksgiving, intercession and petition)

        2. Failure to observe proper prayer protocol (addressed to the Father, in the name of the Son)

        3. Failure to observe proper prayer content (requests outside the confines of the will of God)

3. Outside the Filling of the Holy Spirit

    1. Ephesians 5:18*b* - Be filled with the Holy Spirit.

        Ephesians 6:18 - By means of all intercession and petition, pray at all times in the filling of the Holy

Spirit, being alert to keep praying for all the saints.

BAS-49

4. Ignorance of Bible Doctrine

    1. Rejection of doctrine results in emphasis on wrong priorities.

    2. Rather than pray for what promotes the plan of God you emphasize those things that are expedient for you.

    3. You become involved in what you perceive is pleasing to God rather than learning and doing what He desires.

    4. Isaiah 1:15 - "When you spread out your hands in prayer, I will hide my eyes from you; even if you offer many prayers, I will not listen. Your hands are full of blood.

        Verse 16 - "Wash and make yourselves clean (rebound). Take your evil deeds out of My sight (Stop your production of human good & evil)! Stop doing wrong.

        Verse 17a - "Learn to do right!"

    5. The word for "learn" is the Qal imperative of the verb *lamath*.

    6. In the Piel stem it means "to teach."

    7. The Hebrews felt that each was dependent upon the other and therefore used the same word for both functions.

8. Here the believer is commanded to "Learn." And it might be better translated, "Learn from the process of being taught what is right."

9. In order for your prayers to be answered, you need to pray from an inventory of ideas, not an inventory of ignorance.

5. Under the Control of the Lust Pattern

1. James 4:2 - You lust and do not have what you want, so you commit murder. You are jealous and cannot obtain, so you fight and quarrel. You do not have because you do not ask.

   Verse 3 - You ask and do not receive because you ask with wrong motives, so that you may spend it on pleasures.

2. Lust, murder, jealousy, fighting and quarreling are the wrong ways to get what you want.

3. You should pray for what you want. But if you have the wrong motivation, your prayers won't be answered.

4. The verse says that the lust pattern is the prime motivation for murder.

5. Murder is frustration over not getting what you want.

6. Jealousy is a mental attitude sin which motivates fighting and quarreling.

7. Jealousy is motivated by the fact that another person possesses what we feel rightly belongs to us.

8. Jealousy is directed toward the possessor and feels that if that person were no longer allowed to have the possession then we would.

9. Envy is a much more insidious and dangerous emotional sin.

10. Schoeck, Helmut. *Envy: A Theory of Social Behavior.* (Martin Secker & Warburg Ltd., 1969. Reprint. Indianapolis: Liberty Press, 1987), 20-21:

    A masterly definition and description of envy is found in the *Encyclopedia of Religion and Ethics*, published in 1912. Therein, William L. Davidson, Professor of Logic at the University of Aberdeen has this to say:

    Envy is an emotion that is both selfish and (malicious). It is aimed at persons and implies dislike of one who possesses what the envious man covets or desires. There is in it also a consciousness of inferiority to the person envied. He who has got what I envy is felt by me to have the advantage of me and I resent it. Consequently, I rejoice if he finds that his envied possession does not give him entire satisfaction—(I rejoice) much more if it actually entails on him dissatisfaction and pain: that simply reduces his superiority in my eyes and ministers to my feelings of self-importance...envy is in itself a painful emotion although it is associated with pleasure when misfortune is seen to befall (its) object.

11. It is obvious that uncontrolled mental attitude sins can wreak havoc with one's prayer life.

6. Disobedience to the Mandates of Scripture

    1. 1 John 3:22 - Whatever we have asked we receive from Him because we continue to execute His mandates and we keep on doing what is pleasing in His sight.

    2. From this verse we can see that loyalty to keeping the commands of Scripture is a motivation for God to answer our prayers.

    3. The language in which the New Testament is written is the Koine Greek.

    4. As in all languages, the imperative mood challenges volition.

    5. A command is the expression of God's will directed toward the will of the human soul.

    6. Consequently, the imperative mood does not express reality. There is only probability and possibility.

    7. The emphasis is therefore placed on the volition of the object of the imperative mood.

    8. There are 4 classifications of the imperative mood:

        1. Command: One will make a direct and positive appeal to the will of another.

        2. Prohibition: Used to express a negative command, i.e. "Do not do, etc."

        3. Entreaty: Takes on the force of urgency

or request without the finality of a direct command.

    4.   Permission: This is a command but implies consent on the part of the object.

9.   Failure to submit to these mandates hinders your prayers.

10. For example, failure to:

    a.   Rebound and be filled with the Holy Spirit.
    b.   Utilize the enabling power of the Holy Spirit.
    c.   Consistently take in doctrine.
    d.   Utilize the problem-solving devices to handle the problems of life: Faith-Rest Technique toward circumstances and unconditional love toward people.

7.   Failure to Comply with the Expressed Will of God

1.   1 John 5:14 - This is the confidence which we have face-to-face with Him, that if we ask anything according to His will, He hears us.

2.   The obvious implication is if you do not ask according to His will, He will not hear your prayer.

3.   Knowledge of Bible doctrine is a prerequisite to efficacious prayer.

4.   To pray without knowledge is presumptuous. You assume what is divine policy without really knowing divine policy.

5.   This is similar to No. 4 above but includes those

who are cognizant of what the Bible says but ignore what it says because of pressure or self-centeredness.

6. They know they are asking selfishly but they are so caught up in their problems they feel God will overlook attention to detail.

7. What you really have is a failure to utilize the Faith-Rest Technique and approach the Father free of fear and anxiety.

8. To pray to God while in a state of fear is ludicrous. God conquers fear and you appeal to Him because you are desirous of His help.

9. He desires that your prayers be composed from the inventory of doctrine in your soul, not the emotional ramblings of fear.

10. Knowledge of the will of God can only be acquired by wisdom and spiritual understanding (Colossians 1:9-10).

8. Arrogance

1. Job 35:12 - "They cry out but God does not answer because of the arrogance of evil men."

    Verse 13 - "Surely God will not listen to a phony cry, nor will the Almighty regard it."

2. Arrogance is a system of thought which places self as top priority in life.

3. Arrogant people are always satisfied with themselves but never with others.

4. Such exaggerated preoccupation with self divorces a person from reality.

5. People who are divorced from reality become presumptuous and wrongly assume their ideas to be above reproach simply because they believe them.

6. Their presumptuousness is based on a self-righteous zeal which transforms them into crusaders and reformers.

7. Arrogant, self-righteous priests, who are ignorant of any meaningful biblical scholarship, blindly mislead their followers into disarming themselves and seek to influence the nation to do so. See Isaiah 2:2-4; Micah 4:1-3, compared with Joel 3:9-16; compared with Luke 22:36 and 11:21-22. See Matthew 24:6-7a.

8. Arrogant people are falsely motivated and thus have a false sense of destiny in life.

9. Consequently, it is arrogant to pray for unilateral disarmament, world peace and international harmony.

10. Sadly, those who pursue false destinies are unable to recognize their true destiny when God reveals it to them.

11. Self-righteous people therefore do a lot of praying but their prayers reveal they are more impressed with themselves than with the grace of God.

12. This means their prayers are hindered. Ezekiel 33:13b - "(The righteous man) trusts

in his righteousness and does evil; none of the
righteous things he has done will be remem-
bered."

9. Lack of Compassion

1. Proverbs 21:13 - If man shuts his ears to the cry of
    the poor, he too will cry out and not be answered.

2. There are those who are legitimately destitute in
    that circumstances beyond their control have
    reduced them to poverty.

3. Proper recipients of your compassion would
    include:

    1. Those in poor health due to illness or injury:

        Mark 1:40 - A man with leprosy came to
        (Jesus) and begged Him on his knees, "If you
        are willing, you can make me clean."

        Verse 41 - Filled with compassion, Jesus
        reached out His hand and touched the man.
        "I am willing," He said, "Be clean!"

    2. Those who are handicapped due to birth
        defect or injury:

        Matthew 15:30 - Great crowds came to (Jesus)
        bringing the lame, the blind, the crippled, the
        mute and many others and laid them at His
        feet and He healed them.

        Verse 31 - The people were amazed when
        they saw the mute speaking, the crippled
        made well, the lame walking and the blind

seeing. And they praised the God of Israel.

Verse 32 - Jesus called His disciples to Him and said, "I have compassion for these people; they have already been with Me three days and have nothing to eat."

2 Samuel 9:1-13 - The account of David and Mephibosheth.

3. Those who are persecuted for their faith:

Hebrews 10:32 - Remember those earlier days after you had received the light when you stood your ground in a great contest in the face of suffering.

Verse 33 - Sometimes you were publicly exposed to insult and persecution; at other times you stood side by side with those who were so treated.

Verse 34 - You were compassionate with those in prison and joyfully accepted the confiscation of your property because you knew that yourselves had better and lasting possessions.

4. Those who are widowed or orphaned:

Zechariah 7:8 - And the word of the Lord came to Zechariah,

Verse 9 - "This is what the Lord Omnipotent says, 'Administer true justice. Show mercy and compassion to one another.

Verse 10 - "Do not oppress the widow or the

fatherless, the alien or the poor. In your souls
do not think evil of each other.'"
(Also: James 1:27)

10. Because of Marital Discord

1. 1 Peter 3:7 - Husbands, live with your wives on
the basis of knowledge, she being the weaker vessel since she is a woman, and show respect as a
fellow heir of the grace life so that your prayers
may not be hindered.

BAS-50

2. The husband has a responsibility toward the wife;
show respect.

3. The male of the species was created physically
stronger than the female.

4. The man is thus commanded to execute his
authority over his wife through the application of
Bible doctrine, not through physical force.

5. Secondly, as the weaker vessel, the woman is
designed by God as a responder.

6. The man is designed by God to be the aggressor.

7. Consequently, no man should ever manipulate
his wife by playing to her weaknesses, either
her physical weakness or her subservience as
a responder.

8. It is the husband's responsibility to control every
situation in life through the application of biblical
problem-solving devices.

9. The husband is thus prohibited from manipulating the woman by playing on her emotions or taking advantage of her "responder" instincts.

10. Marriage is Divine Institution Number 2. This union of man and woman forms the basis for an organization called the home.

11. The divinely appointed authority over that organization is the husband (Genesis 3:16b; 1 Corinthians 11:3; Ephesians 5:22; Titus 2:3-5; 1 Peter 3:1.)

12. The divinely imposed foundational policy under which this authority is to function is the command that the husband love his wife with unconditional love. (Ephesians 5:25)

13. The divinely imposed foundational policy for those under His authority is the command that the wife submit to her husband's authority. (Ephesians 5:22)

14. The divinely imposed function for carrying out the husband's policy is that he not be harsh with his wife (Colossians 3:19).

15. The word for "harsh," "bitter," or "embittered" is the present passive imperative of the verb πικραίνω, *pikrainô*.

16. It originally was used by Homer in the *Iliad* for "pointed" or "sharp" as of arrows.

17. Later in the *Odyssey*, Homer used it to describe what is penetrating to the senses or painful to the feelings.

18. Theophrastus (*thêofras'tas*) brought in the concept of bitterness in describing the bitter taste in plants.

19. This concept was later transferred to describe the human soul when it experiences what is unpleasant, unexpected or undesired.

20. The word came to describe anyone who was strict, severe, hostile or cruel.

21. So out of all this came the sense of how the word is used in the New Testament: sternness, severity, bitterness and anger.

22. Ephesians 4:31 finds *pikrainô* at the head of a list of emotional sins:

    Get rid of all *bitterness*, rage, and anger, brawling and slander, along with every form of malice.

23. Here Paul uses it to describe an incensed and angry attitude of mind toward another.

24. Paul uses this same word with the same application in Colossians 3:19 by commanding the husband not to rule his wife through *pikrainô*.

25. The passive voice says that the husband receives the action of the verb.

26. He has allowed something or someone to arouse indignation and anger in his own soul and he is directing his resultant bitterness toward his wife.

27. The wife may be guilty of not measuring up to his standards but that is not an issue.

28. A husband who seeks to change his wife's behavior through arrogance and bitterness will forever fail.

29. As head of the household, he is bound by God to function on divine policy, not personal standards.

30. In any organization, leadership must enforce policy toward those under his responsibility but never personal standards.

31. Leadership husbands motivate their wives through unconditional love which is divine policy.

32. Management husbands intimidate their wives through bitterness and anger because of her violation of his personal standards. 1 Peter 3; 1 Timothy 2

33. Management husbands believe that because wives are responders they have fulfilled their obligation when they issue orders.

34. However, although the wife may obey, she will not respect her husband.

35. Respect and even love will be the motivation of her response if the husband adheres to the divine policy of loving his wife unconditionally.

36. Bible doctrine and personal standards are to be utilized by each individual as he acquires the information.

37. While doctrine remains the same, spiritual growth broadens the inventory of ideas which in turn changes standards.

38. Only doctrine resident in your own soul can

change your standards.

39. The management husband, who superimposes his own standards on his wife, when she has not learned that standard herself from doctrine or has rejected that standard because of doctrine, is a bully and a tyrant.

40. If you have a set of personal standards then you should apply them in your own life. But you should never seek to superimpose them on others including your spouse.

41. The only way another person can change his norms and standards is through spiritual growth.

42. Therefore, if the husband feels his wife's standards are under par with doctrine, he should seek to educate her through unconditional love, compassion and prayer.

43. He cannot force new standards on her. Change must come from within her own soul.

44. Changes in norms and standards which are imposed through tyranny, bullying, intimidation and cruelty are not lasting because they are not inculcated.

45. For a person to change his standards he has to be convinced in his own mind that the new standard is better and why it is better.

46. This can only be properly done through the teaching, learning and acceptance of Bible doctrine in the soul.

47. The husband who fails to recognize this principle and bullies his wife hinders his prayer life.

48. This passage, 1 Peter 3:7, emphasizes the husband. However, the woman can cause a problem as well.

49. When a man exercises his authority under grace and the woman revolts against him, she causes marital discord and her prayers are hindered.

50. Remember the principle: Leadership motivates; management regulates!

CHAPTER TWO
Review: Ten Reasons Why Prayers Go Unanswered

1. Carnality and Cosmic Living (Psalm 66:18; Ephesians 4:30; 1 Thessalonians 5:19)

2. Rejection of Divine Policy (rebound, thanksgiving, intercession and petition addressed to the Father in the name of Jesus Christ within the framework of the plan of God.)

3. Outside the Filling of the Holy Spirit (Ephesians 5:18; 6:18)

4. Ignorance of Bible Doctrine (Isaiah 1:15-17)

5. Under the Control of the Lust Pattern of the Sin Nature (James 4:2-3)

6. Disobedience to the Mandates of Scripture (1 John 3:22)

7. Failure to Comply to the Expressed Will of God (1 John 5:14; Colossians 1:9-10)

8. Arrogance (Job 35:12-13; Ezekiel 33:13)

9. Lack of Compassion (Proverbs 21:13; Mark 1:40-41; Matthew 15:30-32; 2 Samuel 9:1-13; Hebrews 10:32-34; Zechariah 7:8-10)

10. Marital Discord (1 Peter 3:7; Colossians 3:19)

CHAPTER THREE
Review of Doctrines

Following, is a review of what we have covered:

1. God exists and He has a plan for you.

2. That plan has three phases:

   a. Phase 1: Salvation
   b. Phase 2: The Christian Way of Life
   c. Phase 3: The Eternal State

3. The Trinity: Father, Son and Holy Spirit.

4. The Essence of God

   1. Sovereignty. God is our absolute Authority.
   2. Righteousness. God is our absolute Standard.
   3. Justice. God is the absolute Judge.
   4. Love. God is the absolute Benefactor.
   5. Eternal Life. God is the absolute Being.
   6. Omniscience. God is the absolute Intellect.
   7. Omnipotence. God is the absolute Power.
   8. Omnipresence. God is the absolute Eyewitness.
   9. Immutability. God is the absolute Stabilizer.
   10. Veracity. God is our absolute Counselor.

5. The Three Personalities of the Trinity:

   1. Diety of the Father
   2. Diety of Jesus Christ
   3. Deity of the Holy Spirit

6. The fall of Man in the Garden of Eden. (Genesis 3)

    1. Demon Influence from Satan's Cosmic System
    2. Subsequent Negative Volition
    3. Resultant Spiritual Death
    4. The Barrier
    5. Reconciliation (Christ removes the Barrier)

7. Nine False Approaches to Salvation

    1. Repenting of your sins. Sins are not the issue but rather, "What think ye of Christ?"

    2. Making a commitment to Jesus Christ. This is human energy. All that is required is to believe.

    3. Lordship Salvation or proving you are really saved by your good works. Divine Good is the result of spiritual growth. Salvation is the result of faith alone in Christ alone.

    4. Ritual Salvation, i.e., believe plus be baptized , be circumcised, observe the Eucharist, keep the Law. Salvation is by faith alone in Christ alone. Ritual without reality is meaningless.

    5. Morality. Salvation is available only to those who believe in Christ. Morality is available to all humanity, believer and unbeliever alike.

    6. Salvation by Emotion. You are not saved because you feel saved. You are saved through faith alone in Christ alone.

    7. Church Membership. An illogical claim. James was a believer before he founded the first church in Jerusalem. James believed in Christ and later

formed the original local church.

8. Psychological Works. This is faith plus group activity, i.e., public profession of repentance, walking the aisle. Salvation is through belief in Christ. You may do this in the privacy of your own soul.

9. Reverse Invitation. Inviting Christ into your heart or life. Offering an invitation to Christ as an unbeliever is like inviting Queen Elizabeth over for hot dogs. God invites you to His house through faith alone in Christ alone.

8. The Biblical Word for Faith and Believe—πίστις, *pistis*

1. The noun form is translated into the English as "faith," while the verb form as "believe."

2. Scriptural documentation of salvation by means of faith alone in Christ alone:

    John 3:15-18, 36; 6:47; 11:25; 20:31; Acts 16:31; Romans 1:16; 3:22, 28; Galatians 2:16; 3:26; 1 John 5:11-13; Ephesians 2:8-9.

9. Spirituality: A status in which the Holy Spirit controls the thinking of the believer who is in fellowship.

1. Lust Pattern of the Old Sin Nature
2. Confession of sin: ὁμολογέω, *homologeô*
3. Classification of sin
    a. Mental Attitude
    b. Verbal or Sins of the Tongue
    c. Overt
4. Human Good: Any good deed performed outside the Bottom Circle.

5. Evil: Any energy-of-the-flesh activity which seeks to solve the problems of life apart from the leadership of the Word of God.

10. Parable of the Prodigal Son (Luke 15:11-32)

1. Sonship (Verse 11)
2. Personal sin and carnality
3. Divine Operating Assets (Verse 12)
4. Far Country or life in the Cosmic System (Verse 13)
5. Ramifications from poor decisions (famine) (Verse 14)
6. Poor decisions limit future options (A Jew works for a Gentile pig farmer) (Verse 15)
7. Logistical Grace never stops (although pig slop is a long way from the grain-fattened calf) (Verse 16)
8. Holy Spirit's motivation to rebound (Verse 17)
9. Rebound recovery (Verse 18)
10. Penance is not grace (Verse 19)
11. Compassion of divine grace (Verse 20)
12. Prodigal's reiteration of rebound adjustment (Verse 21)
13. Divine response to the rebound prayer (restoration to fellowship) (Verses 22-23)
14. Divine joy over repentant believer (Doctrine of Deaths; #6: Temporal Death) (Verse 24)
15. The Elder Brother compared to the self-righteous Pharisees (Verse 25-27; Matthew 23:1-33; 22:1-14)
16. Sin of Anger
    Doctrine of the Old Sin Nature
    a. Strength: Human Good
    b. Weakness: Personal Sin
    c. Trends
       1. Asceticism (self-righteousness)
       2. Lasciviousness (Antinomianism)

    d. Lust Pattern
       1. Power
       2. Approbation
       3. Hedonism
       4. Murder
       5. Anger
       6. Monetary
    e. The Old Sin Nature is a grenade and volition is the firing pin
    f. Pre-salvation sin solved at the cross
    g. Post-salvation sin solved by rebound

17. Refusal to rebound causes one to fragment into the Cosmic System (self-righteousness; self-pity; self-justification; bitterness, lying; judging; arrogance of believing that your works warrant special treatment from God (Verses 29-30)

18. Salvation is eternal and rebound is always available. (Verses 31-32)

11. The Importance of Doctrine (6 points)

12. Doctrine of Grace Apparatus for Perception (1 Corinthians 2:4-14)

13. Doctrine of Dispensations

    A. Theocentric
       1. Gentiles
       2. Israel

    B. Christocentric
       1. Incarnation
       2. Church

    C. Eschatological
       1. Tribulation
       2. Millennium

14. Doctrine of the Mysteries of the Church Age
    1. Baptism of the Holy Spirit
    2. Perfect Environment of the Bottom Circle
    3. Royal Priesthood
    4. Royal Ambassadorship
    5. Citizenship in Heaven
    6. Royal Aristocracy

15. Doctrine of the Faith-Rest Drill

    1. Introduction from Exodus 17:1-7 and Numbers 20:2-11
    2. Hebrews 3:7-4:3
    3. The Mechanics of the Faith-Rest Drill
       a. Stage 1: Claiming Promises
       b. Stage 2: Doctrinal Rationales:
          1. Essence of God
          2. Plan of God
          3. Logistical Grace Support
       c. Stage 3: Doctrinal Conclusions
    4. Biblical Example from Genesis 17:16-19 compared with Romans 4:19-21
       a. Principles of Discipline and Suffering
          1. Law of Volitional Responsibility
          2. Law of Divine Discipline
          3. Principle of Suffering for Blessing
    5. Literary Illustration from William McGuffey's *Fifth Eclectic Reader*: "The Righteous Never Forsaken."

16. Principles of Discipline and Suffering

    1. Law of Volitional Responsibility
    2. Law of Divine Discipline
    3. Principle of Suffering for Blessing

17. Doctrine of Prayer

   1. Biblical Vocabulary for Prayer
   2. The Four Paragraphs of Biblical Prayer
   3. Proper Prayer Content
   4. Special Prayers
   5. Ten Reasons Why Prayers Are Not Answered

18. You have now completed the *'89 Basics Series* study. You are now ready for the advanced classes. If you are the average learner and own a good dictionary, you can advance in these Bible classes. You may not completely understand all that you hear, but the Holy Spirit will instruct you based on what you have already learned. Your spiritual growth will be slow but steady, just like the rest of us. The objective is to grow a little every day, one day at a time.

4354445444

444

44444544

Scripture Index

OLD TESTAMENT

GENESIS
Genesis 1:29 23
Genesis 3 56
Genesis 3:16 49
Genesis 9:2 23
Genesis 9:3 23
Genesis 15:6 28
Genesis 17:16-19 60

EXODUS
Exodus 17: 1-7 60

NUMBERS
Numbers 20:2-11 60

DEUTERONOMY
Deuteronomy 30:11-14 30

2 SAMUEL
2 Samuel 9:1-13 . . . . 47, 54

JOB
Job 35:12 44
Job 35:12-13 54
Job 35:13 44

PSALMS
Psalm 66:18 . . . . 10, 37, 54

PROVERBS
Proverbs 21:13 . . . . 46, 54

ISAIAH
Isaiah 1:15 39
Isaiah 1:15-17 54
Isaiah 1:16 39
Isaiah 1:17a 39
Isaiah 2:2-4 45
Isaiah 8:14 28
Isaiah 26:16 28

EZEKIEL
Ezekiel 33:13 . . . . 45, 54

JOEL
Joel 3:9-16 45

MICAH
Micah 4:1-3 45

ZECHARIAH
Zechariah 7:8 47
Zechariah 7:8-10 54
Zechariah 7:9 47
Zechariah 7:10 47

NEW TESTAMENT

MATTHEW
Matthew 5:44 35
Matthew 6:9 3
Matthew 15:30 46
Matthew 15:30-32 54
Matthew 15:31 46
Matthew 15:32 47
Matthew 22:1-14 58
Matthew 23:1-33 58
Matthew 24: 6-7 45

MARK
Mark 1:40 46
Mark 1:40-41 54
Mark 1:41 46
Mark 11:24 20

LUKE
Luke 11:21-22 45
Luke 15:11-32 58
Luke 22:36 45

JOHN
John 3:15-16 33
John 3:15-18 57
John 3:18 33
John 3:36 . . . . v, 33, 57
John 6:47 . . . . 33, 57
John 9:31 10
John 11:25 . . . . 33, 57
John 14:13-14 3
John 15:7 . . . . 19, 21
John 17:1 3
John 20:31 . . . . 33, 57

ACTS
Acts 16:31 . . . . 33, 57

ROMANS
Romans 1:16 . . . . 33, 57
Romans 1:21 11
Romans 3:22 . . . . 33, 57
Romans 3:28 . . . . 33, 57
Romans 4:1 28
Romans 4:1-5 33
Romans 4:2 28
Romans 4:3 28
Romans 4:4 29
Romans 4:5 29
Romans 4:19-21 60

Romans 8:27 6
Romans 9-11 . . . . .26, 27, 34
Romans 9:30 27
Romans 9:31 28
Romans 9:32 28
Romans 9:33 28
Romans 10:1 29
Romans 10:2 29
Romans 10:3 29
Romans 10:4 30
Romans 10:8 30
Romans 10:8-11 .33
Romans 10:9 .30, 33
Romans 10:9-10 . . . . .26, 33
Romans 10:10 . . . . .30, 33
Romans 10:11 33
Romans 12:10 9

1 CORINTHIANS
1 Corinthians 2:4-14 59
1 Corinthians 10:13 18
1 Corinthians 11:3 49
1 Corinthians 11:31 10
1 Corinthians 13:4-8 16

2 CORINTHIANS
2 Corinthians 9:11 5
2 Corinthians 10:4 16
2 Corinthians 10:5 17
2 Corinthians 10:6 17

GALATIANS
Galatians 2:16 . . . . .33, 57
Galatians 3:26 . . . . .33, 57

EPHESIANS
Ephesians 1:16 12
Ephesians 1:17 13
Ephesians 1:18 13
Ephesians 2:8-9 . . . . .33, 57
Ephesians 4:30 . . . . .37, 54
Ephesians 4:31 50
Ephesians 5:18 . . . . .38, 54
Ephesians 5:20 5
Ephesians 5:20a 3, 5
Ephesians 520b 3
Ephesians 5:22 49
Ephesians 5:25 49
Ephesians 6:18 . . . . .4, 7, 8, 20, 38, 54

PHILIPPIANS
Philippians 1:3 13
Philippians 1:4 13
Philippians 1:5 13
Philippians 1:6 13
Philippians 1:9 35
Philippians 3:5 26
Philippians 4:6 . . . . .5, 7, 8, 11
Philippians 4:11 12

Philippians 4:12 12
Philippians 4:13 12

COLOSSIANS
Colossians 1:7-8 13
Colossians 1:9 . . . . .13, 35
Colossians 1:9-10 . . . . .44, 54
Colossians 1:10 . . . . .14, 15
Colossians 1:11 . . . . .14, 15
Colossians 1:12 . . . . .14, 15
Colossians 3:12 18
Colossians 3:19 . . . . .49, 50, 54
Colossians 3:22 18
Colossians 4:2 . . . . .18, 36
Colossians 4:3 37

1 THESSALONIANS
1 Thessalonians 5:17 4
1 Thessalonians 5:18 12
1 Thessalonians 5:19 . . . . .38, 54

2 THESSALONIANS
2 Thessalonians 3:1 36

1 TIMOTHY
1 Timothy 2 51
1 Timothy 2:1 23
1 Timothy 2:2 24
1 Timothy 2:3 24
1 Timothy 4:4 22
1 Timothy 4:5 22

2 TIMOTHY
2 Timothy 3:1 11
2 Timothy 3:2 11

TITUS
Titus 2:3-5 49
Titus 3:5 34

HEBREWS
Hebrews 3:7-4:3 60
Hebrews 7:25 . . . . .6, 20
Hebrews 10:32 47
Hebrews 10:32-34 54
Hebrews 10:33 47
Hebrews 10:34 47
Hebrews 13:18 36

JAMES
James 1:27 48
James 4:2 40
James 4:2-3 54
James 4:3 40

1 PETER
1 Peter 3 51
1 Peter 3:1 49
1 Peter 3:7 . . . . .48, 53, 54

1 Peter 3:12 7

1 JOHN

1 John 1:9 . . . . .v, 4, 10
1 John 2:1*b* 6
1 John 3:22 . . . . .42, 54
1 John 5:11-13 . . . . .33, 57
1 John 5:14 . . . . .20, 54

JUDE

Jude 20 4

REVELATION

Revelation 12:10 6

Subject Index

Aberdeen, University of, 41
Abraham, 28
Advocate, 5
Agenda for prayer, 19
Aggressor, 48
Anger, 51
Anxiety, 44
Arrogance, 32, 51, 54
Arrogance complex, 38
Arrogant, 45
Authority, 49
BAS-44, 3
BAS-45, 9
BAS-46, 15
BAS-47, 23
BAS-48, 31
BAS-49, 39
BAS-50, 48
Believe, 20, 57
Bitterness, 50, 51
Bottom Circle, 37
Carnality, 54
Christian way of life, 55
Christocentric, 59
Claim a promise, 18
Client nation, 24
Compassion, 52
Compassion, lack of, 54
Confess, 4
Cosmic Living, 54
Cosmic Systems, 38
Crusaders, 45
David, 47
Davidson, William L., 41
Disaster testing, 18
Disobedience, 54
Dispensations, 59
Divine Institution Number 2, 49
Divine policy, 43, 51, 54
Doctrinal conclusion, 18
Doctrine, 36, 44
    importance of, 59
Eden, 56
'89 Basics Series, 1, 10, 61
Emotional sins, 50
Encyclopedia of Religion and Ethics, 41
Envy: A Theory of Social Behavior, 41
Eschatological, 59
Essence of God, 25, 55
Essence of God Rationale, 18
Eternal life, 27
Eternal state, 55
Evangelists, 37
Evil, 58
Failure, 54
Faith, 33, 34, 57

Faith alone, 29, 34, 57
Faith-Rest Drill, 60
Faith-Rest Technique, 4, 17, 18, 43, 44
Fall, 56
False destinies, 45
False sense of destiny, 45
Father, 9
Fear, 44
Fellowship, 57
Filling of the Holy Spirit, 4, 9, 54
Financial Policy, 2
GAP (Grace Apparatus for Perception), 59
Gentiles, 27
God
    the Father, 20
    sovereignty, 25
Gospel, 25, 32
Grace, 34
Grace Apparatus for Perception (GAP), 59
Grace of God, 34
Handicapped, 46
Harsh, 49
Hatred complex, 38
Holy Spirit, 6, 20, 31, 36, 43, 61
Home, 49
Homer, 49
Horton, Gary, 37
Hughes, Rick, 37
Husband, 48, 49, 50, 51, 53
Ignorance, 54
Iliad, 49
Imperative Mood, 42
Imperative Mood Command, 42
Imperative Mood Entreaty, 42
Imperative Mood Permission, 43
Imperative Mood Prohibition, 42
Intercession, 3, 5, 8, 12
Inventory of ideas, 51
Israel's
    acceptance, 27
    rejection, 27
    selection, 27
Jealousy, 41
Jehovah, 32
Jesus Christ, 3, 20, 28, 30
    in the name of, 9
Jewish unbeliever, 34
Jurisprudence, 24
Justice of God, 25
KJV (King James Version), 6
Klein, Max, 37
Koine Greek, 42
Kurios, 32
LaRosa, Ralph, 37
Leadership, 51
    husbands, 51

Learn, 39
Lord, 32
Love, 49, 51
Loyalty, 42
Luke 15:11-32, 58
Lust pattern, 40, 54
Management husband(s), 51, 52
Marital discord, 53, 54
Marriage, 49
McGuffey, William, 60
McGuffey's Fifth Eclectic Reader, 60
Mephibosheth, 47
Messiah, 27, 29, 32, 33
Military preparedness, 24
Missionaries, 37
Mosaic Law, 27
Moses, 30, 31
Motivation, 36, 42
Murder, 40
Mysteries of the Church Age, 60
Nine false approaches to salvation, 56
Norms and standards, 17, 52
Odyssey, 49
Onwubiko, Moses, 37
Orphaned, 47
Painful, 49
Parenthesis, 26, 27
Pastors, 37
Paul, 27, 28, 29, 30, 31, 33
People testing, 16
Persecuted, 47
Personal Love for God, 11
Personal standards, 51
Petition, 3, 6, 8, 15
Pistis, 57
Pivot, 24
Plan of God Rationale, 18
Policy, 49
Poor health, 46
Positive volition, 35, 36
Prayer(s), 3, 7, 8, 11, 19, 52
    effectiveness of 21
    proper content 38
    proper procedure 38
    proper protocol, 38
    protocol, 19
    why not answered
        arrogance, 44
        carnality and cosmic living, 37
        disobedience to the mandates of
            scripture, 42
        failure to comply with the expressed
            will of God, 43
        ignorance of Bible Doctrine, 39
        lack of compassion, 46
        marital discord, 48
        outside the filling of the Holy Spirit, 38
        rejection of Divine Policy, 38
        under the control of the Lust Pattern, 40

Problem-solving device, 16, 35, 43, 48
Prodigal Son, 58
Public profession of faith, 26
Racial Jew, 27
Rebound, 3, 9, 10, 16, 18, 43
Reformers, 45
Request, 7, 8
Respect, 51
Responder, 48
Rewards and blessings, 36
Righteous Never Forsaken, The, 60
Righteousness, 27
    imputed, 27
Romans 9-11, 26
Salvation, 27, 31, 33, 34, 55
Savior, 34
Schoeck, Helmut, 41
Second Advent, 28
Self-centeredness, 44
Self-righteousness, 29
Sin Nature, 54
Special prayers, 22
Special prayers, for
    communicators of truth 36
    fellow believers' spiritual adulthood 35
    the unbeliever 24
    those in authority 23
    your enemies 35
Special prayers over meals, 22
Spiritual growth, 52, 61
Spiritual Jew, 27
Spiritual maturity, 15, 36
Spiritual understanding, 44
Spirituality, 57
Standards, 52
Suffering for blessing, 16
Swafford, Quentin, 37
System testing, 17, 18
Teach, 39
Thanksgiving, 3, 11, 12
Thanksgivings, 4, 10
Theocentric, 59
Theophrastus, 50
Thought testing, 16
Trinity, 55
True destiny, 45
Unconditional love, 16, 17, 35, 43, 49, 51, 52
    toward mankind 12
Virtue love, 12
Volition, 24, 26, 42
Volitional choice, 26, 33
Widowed, 47
Wife, 48, 51, 53
Will of God, 44
Wisdom, 44
Works, 27, 31, 34
Worry, 18
Wrong motivation, 40
Wrong priorities, 39

Notes

Notes

Notes

Notes

Notes